Adventures With Papa

By

Keidra McGriff

Copyright © 2022 BFF Publishing House, LLC

Printed in the United States of America

Email: Burginkeidra@gmail.com

ISBN: 979-8-9864642-5-1

All rights reserved. No part of this book may be reproduced or used in any manner without written permission of the author, except for the use of quotations in a book review.

BFF Publishing House is a Limited Liability Corporation dedicated wholly to the appreciation and publication of children and adults for the advancement of diversification in literature.

For more information on publishing contact

Antionette Mutcherson at

bff@bffpublishinghouse.com

Website: bffpublishinghouse.com

Published in the United States by

BFF Publishing House

Atlanta, Ga. First Edition, 2022

Dedicated to:

Keenan, Kobe, and Daddy to me; Papa Keith to them.
May he rest peacefully.

Keith Leon Burgin
November 24, 1952-December 6, 2018

Ad·ven·ture: an exciting or remarkable experience

I always looked forward to Saturday mornings with Papa.

Papa would knock on the window next to the back door.

His knock was so loud that I always knew when it was him.

When he came in the house, he would loudly say,

"Come here, boy, give your Papa a hug."

If he didn't have them already, he would go get my favorite thing to eat on Saturday mornings: DONUTS! Glazed with blue icing and sprinkles… mmm, mmm, good!

After we ate, our weekend adventures would begin.

Papa and I would do some of everything.

One time, he hooked a buggy up to the back of his lawnmower and drove it all around the backyard.

Everybody who drove down the street honked their horns and laughed at us.

Papa loved his lawnmower and had a passion for a good-looking lawn.

He mowed the neighbors' lawns with his cool, bright yellow lawnmower.

It was always exciting to see the lawns before and after.

Something else Papa loved was fishing.

He took me fishing at the lake once.

He taught me how to hook the bait and cast my line.

We didn't catch anything that day, but I sure did have fun at the lake, fishing with Papa.

Papa took my mommy fishing when she was little, like me.

My Papa could fix anything. He had so many tools.

He showed me how to use his tools to fix my toys when they were broken.

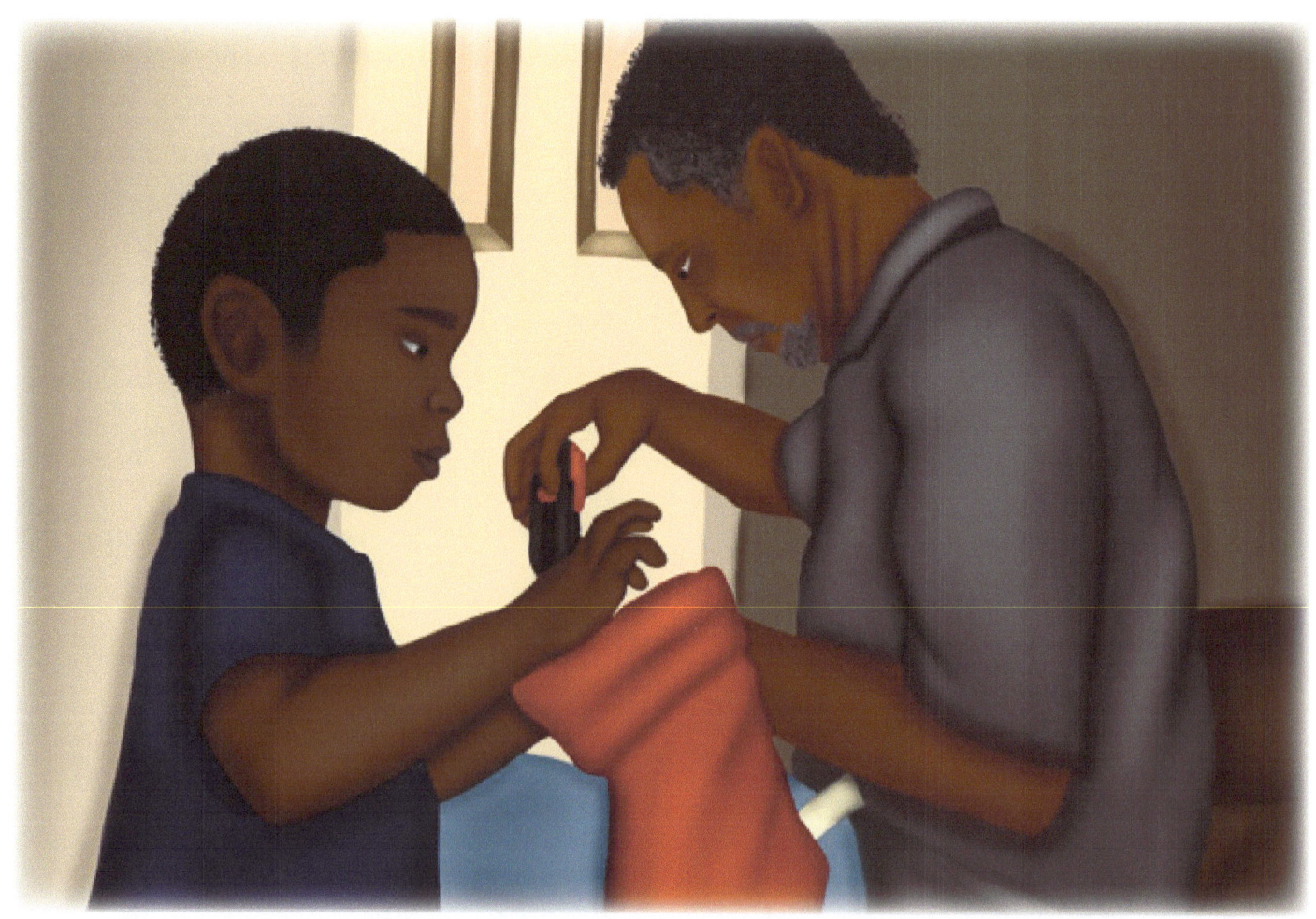

It was always a learning adventure, fixing things with Papa.

Mommy called Papa "Fred Sanford."

I don't even know who Fred Sanford is!

Mommy told me, "He's a guy from TV. He was a junk dealer and collected lots and lots of stuff, just like Papa."

Papa wasn't a junk dealer, but he had lots and lots of stuff, too.

I can't imagine anybody having as much stuff as Papa.

He always had LOTS of junk!

One person's junk is another person's treasure.

Papa always brought treasures for me and my cousins.

He brought us treasures, like bikes and scooters.

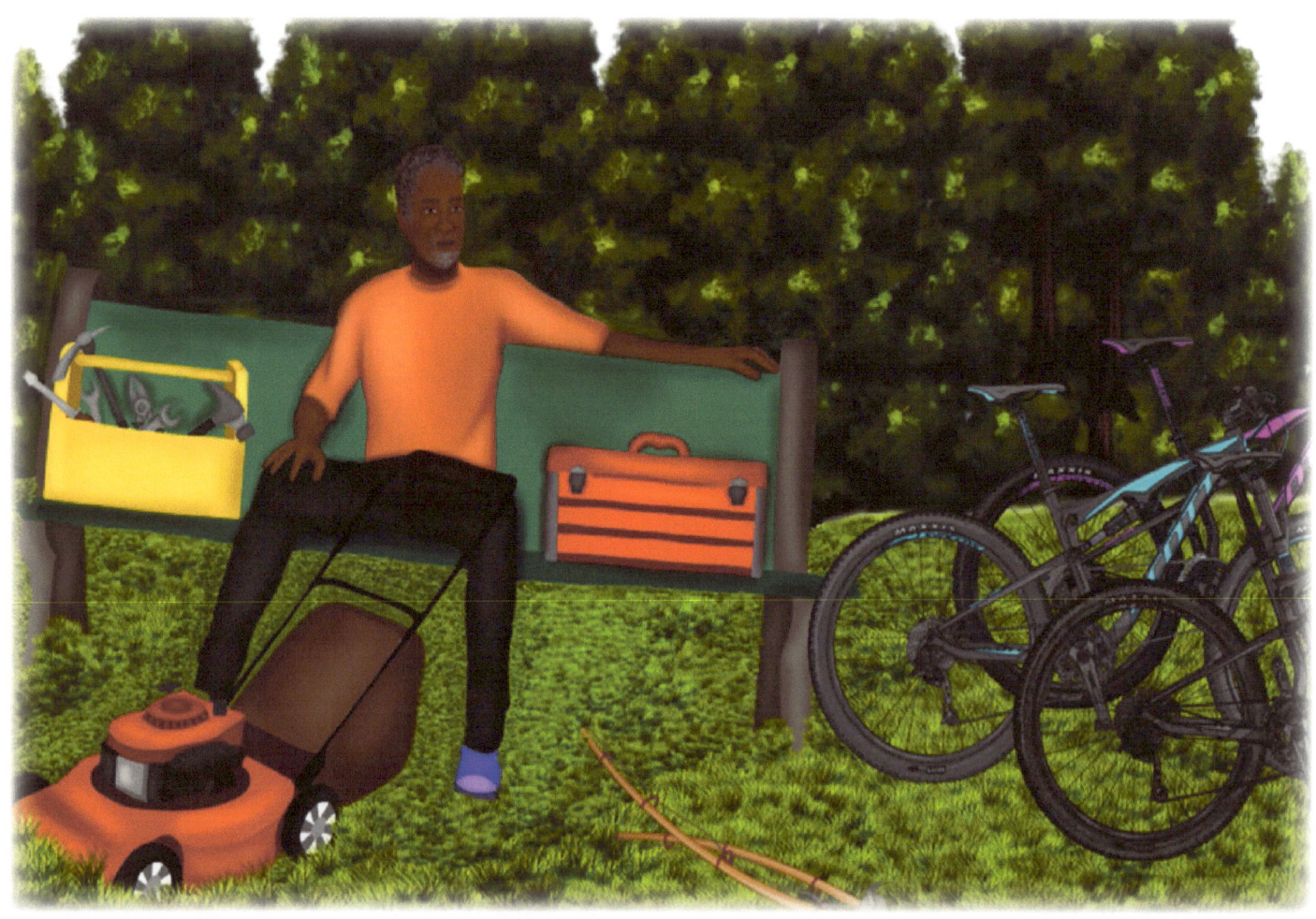

He also built a swing set in the backyard.

I like to slide down the slide really, really fast!

Everybody in the neighborhood knows Papa!

It's like he's a neighborhood celebrity.

They should name a street after him.

Neighbors trusted him with everything, even their dogs!

He would walk right into their backyards and bring their dogs to me.

He taught me to not be scared of dogs.

When I was with Papa, I wasn't scared of the dogs or anything!

On one of our last adventures together, we rode go-karts.

Papa drove the go-kart and I rode with him.
We were looping and zooming super fast around the track.

We had so much fun!

Every day with Papa was the BEST DAY EVER!

Now, Papa plays in Heaven with God and watches over me.

He and God have adventures together.

I hope Papa is telling God and his friends in Heaven about me, the same way I tell everybody about him.

I will tell my little brother all about our Papa and all of our adventures.

I wish everybody had a Papa like my Papa Keith!

Now, our adventures are in my dreams and memories,

and I will cherish them forever.

Keidra McGriff

Keidra Burgin-McGriff initially wanted to write a children's book with a family that looks like hers, but did not have an actual story in mind. The only goal at the time was to diversify bookshelves with a relatable story. After her father's unexpected passing, she wanted to preserve her son's memories of his papa. From there, *Adventures with Papa* was born.

Keidra is a full-time attorney and resides in the Dallas area with her husband and two sons. She is a proud two-time HBCU Alumna and member of Alpha Kappa Alpha Sorority, Incorporated.

www.ingramcontent.com/pod-product-compliance
Lightning Source LLC
LaVergne TN
LVHW072100070426
835508LV00002B/193